How to Hold Scissors

Insert your thumb into the smaller opening of the scissors. Then insert your index finger and middle finger (in some cases, your ring finger as well) into the larger opening.

Base of the scissors

★ The base of the scissors is where the two blades meet.

★ Use scissors with rounded points and edges.

Thumb
(Right before first joint)

Index finger

Middle finger

★ Use child-sized scissors that are easy to open and close.

How to Use Scissors

When using scissors, the elbow of the arm that is holding the scissors should be touching the body at the waist. Scissors should be held straight out from the body, and the paper should be held perpendicular to the scissors.

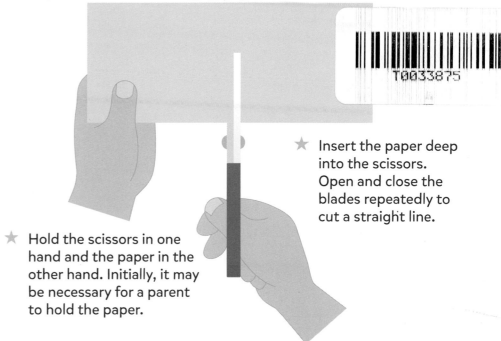

★ Insert the paper deep into the scissors. Open and close the blades repeatedly to cut a straight line.

★ Hold the scissors in one hand and the paper in the other hand. Initially, it may be necessary for a parent to hold the paper.

CAUTION

■ Always carry scissors by the handle, CLOSED, and blades DOWN.

■ When handing scissors to someone, hold the CLOSED blades in your hand and pass them off with the HANDLE OUT.

■ Don't cut anything but paper with scissors.

■ Always sit down when using scissors.

■ Don't touch the sharp edge of the scissor blades.

■ Don't point scissors at living things.

Hold the glue stick between the middle finger, index finger, and thumb. 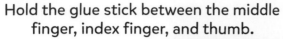 **1**

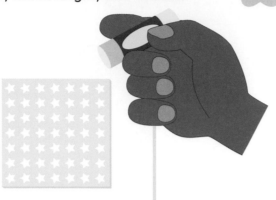

Apply glue to the edges of the paper. **2**

★ Place a larger piece of paper under the one you're gluing to protect your work surface.

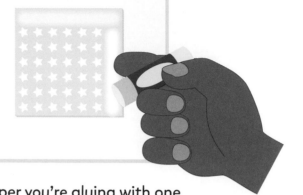

★ Hold the piece of paper you're gluing with one hand and the glue stick with the other.

Apply glue to the middle of the paper. **3**

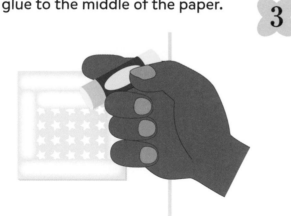

Now you are ready to turn over the paper with the glue and place it in its place. **4**

There are many types of glue (glue stick, liquid glue, rubber cement). In school, a glue stick is more common. The method for applying glue is pretty much the same no matter which type of glue is used.

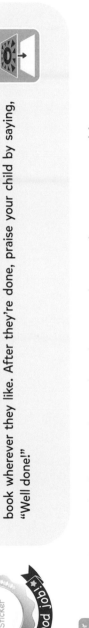

Play with Dogs

Let's play with dogs. Place the dog stickers wherever you like.

Good job!

Sticker

3

Put Stars in the Sky

To Parents: Have your child apply the star stickers wherever they like. After they're done, praise your child by saying, "You made such a beautiful night sky!"

Good job!

Sticker

 Place the ☆ stickers in the night sky.

4

Add Blossoms to the Tree

To Parents: In this activity, your child will practice applying a sticker to a limited area. Encourage them or her to keep the stickers in the green area of the tree and to not overlap other petals.

Sticker

sticker

Place the ❀ stickers on the tree.

Match the Animals

To Parents: Use the pink signs to decide where to place the matching animal stickers. Praise your child by saying, "Well done!" when they apply the stickers within the pens.

 Let's put each animal in its pen. Place the matching animal sticker in its ◯.

Play with Building Blocks

To Parents: In this activity, your child will practice placing a sticker on a specific area. Have your child apply each sticker to its matching light blue area as accurately as possible. Then ask, "What did the boy and girl make?"

The children are building with blocks. Let's help them.
Apply each building block sticker on its matching shape.

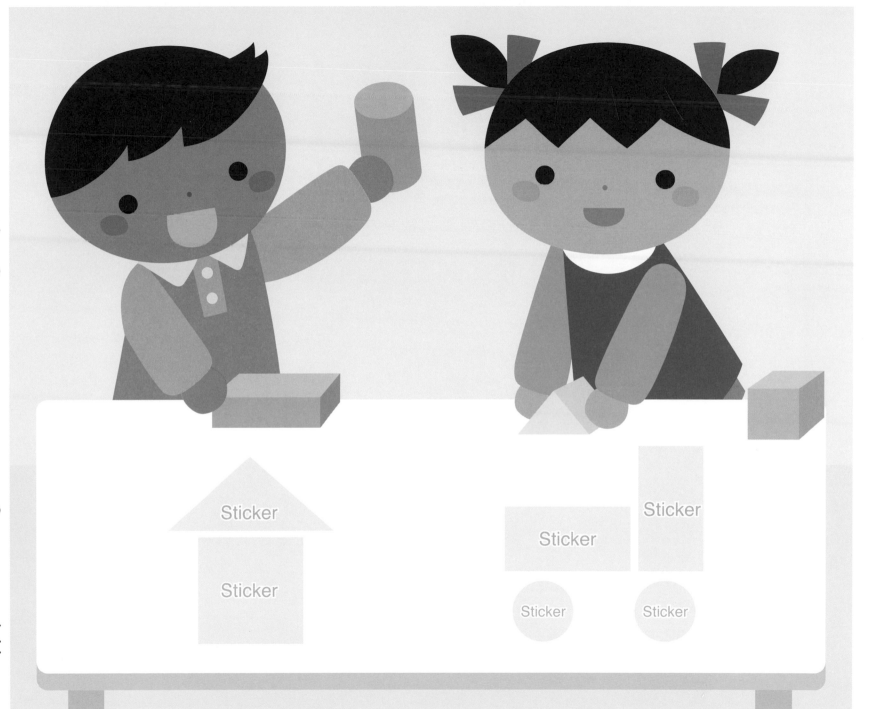

Sticker

Sticker

Sticker

Sticker

Sticker

Sticker

Read the Traffic Signals

To Parents: Discuss each traffic signal and what it means. Ask, "What color is the traffic signal when it is okay to cross the street?" and "What color is the signal when you must wait to cross the street?"

Good job!

What does the traffic signal show when it is safe to cross the street? Apply the traffic signal stickers to match each picture.

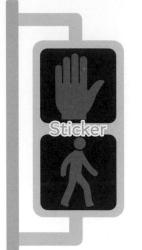

Sticker

Sticker

Watch the Fireworks

To Parents: Starting with this activity, your child will practice cutting straight lines. Cut the thin lines for your child before they cut the thick lines. Then have them place the cutouts on the page before gluing the pieces in place.

Sticker

Good job!

Cut out the fireworks. Glue them onto the picture wherever you like.

Parents: Cut this line for your child.

Catch Bugs

To Parents: It is very difficult for young children to cut long, straight lines. Your child should cut the short, thick lines. However, if your child wants to cut the long lines, allow them to try.

Sticker

★ Good job! ★

Cut out the bugs. Glue them onto the picture wherever you like.

Glue

Glue

Glue

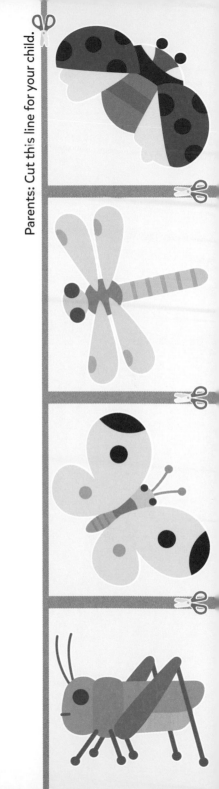

Glue

Glue

Glue

Glue

Plant Flowers

To Parents: In the beginning, your child may have difficulty with gluing. As shown on page 2, place a large piece of paper underneath for gluing. After your child is done, praise them by saying, "It's a beautiful garden."

Sticker

Good job!

Cut out the flowers. Glue them on the garden patch wherever you like.

Parents: Cut this line for your child.

Glue

Glue

Glue

Glue

Make a Busy Road

To Parents: The vehicles face either left or right. Encourage your child to pay attention to the direction the vehicles are going when deciding where to place them on the road. After your child glues the vehicles in place, ask, "What kind of vehicles are driving on the road?"

Sticker

Good job!

Cut out all the vehicles. Glue them in place to make a busy road.

Parents: Cut this line for your child.

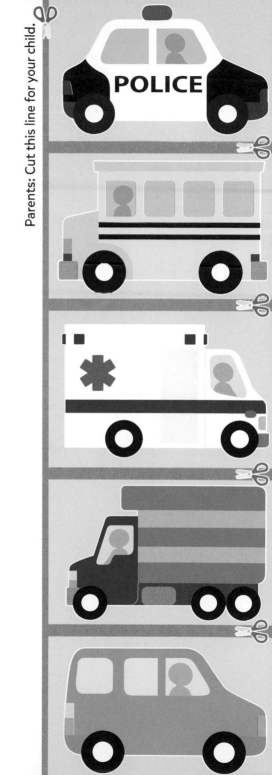

Glue
Glue
Glue
Glue
Glue

Get Dressed

To Parents: This might be difficult for your child because there isn't a specific area to place the cutouts. Have your child make a habit of placing each cutout on a picture before gluing to make sure it's in the best position.

Sticker

★ Good job! ★

Let's help these kids put on their clothes.
Cut out all the clothes and glue them in place.

Parents: Cut these thin lines for your child.

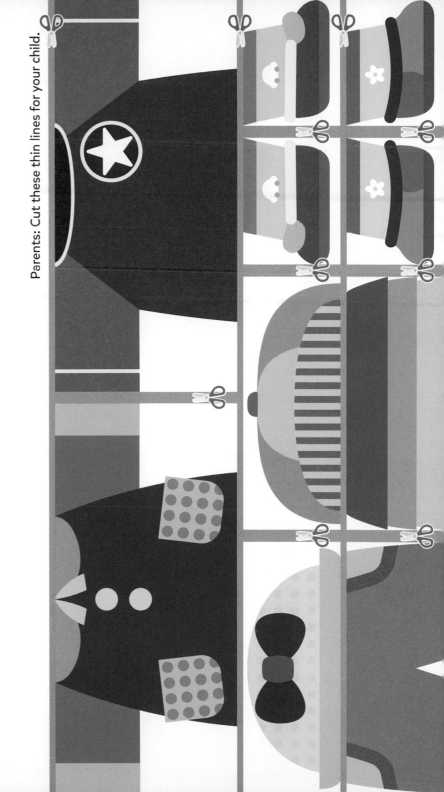

Glue Glue Glue Glue Glue Glue Glue Glue Glue Glue Glue Glue

Go to School

To Parents: Each bridge is different in size and shape. Have your child put the cutouts in place before gluing them onto the picture. Even though your child may put one in the right place, they may have it upside down. Tell your child to pay attention to the direction and glue them.

Cut out the bridges. Then use the shadows inside [ ] to decide where to glue each matching bridge. Follow the road from ↑ to ↑ to get to school.

Good job!

Sticker

PRESCHOOL

SCHOOL BUS

Play on the Playground

To Parents: Your child can practice cutting long lines, which requires them to open and close the scissors repeatedly. But if your child has difficulty, cut halfway for them and let them cut the rest. When finished gluing the cutouts in place, ask, "What is the name of this?"

Sticker

★ Good job! ★

Cut out the playground equipment. Then use the shadows inside [ ] to decide where to glue the matching pieces.

Glue

Glue

Glue

Glue

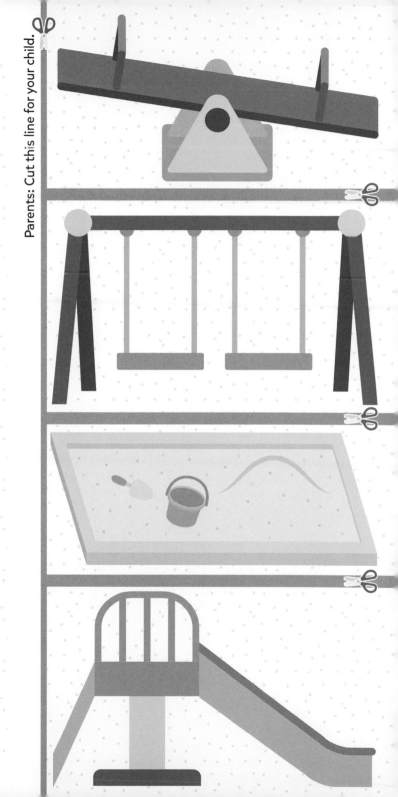

Parents: Cut this line for your child.

Match the Patterns

To Parents: Cut out and put each pattern on the correct animal. When your child places the cutouts, have them pay attention to colors and patterns. Pasting pieces upside down is okay. After your child has finished the task, ask them to name each animal.

Let's match the patterns.
Cut out the patterns and glue the matching pieces on   .

Parents: Cut this line for your child.

Do not use.

23

Glue

Glue

Glue

Glue

Do not use.

Finish the Faces

To Parents: In this activity, your child will practice cutting out small pieces. Cutting short lines many times is good practice for opening and closing scissors repeatedly. Sort out the eye, nose, and mouth pieces and place them on the pictures.

Good job!

Sticker

24

Cut out the face parts. Then glue them onto Rabbit's and Bear's faces.

Make an Aquarium

To Parents: Your child doesn't have to count fish if it is difficult for them. Have your child check which tank has more fish. Then place the same shape or number of fish on the paper to match the shadows before gluing.

Cut out the fish. Then glue them in each fish tank to match their shadows. Add the sea creature stickers to the tanks.

Good job!

Sticker

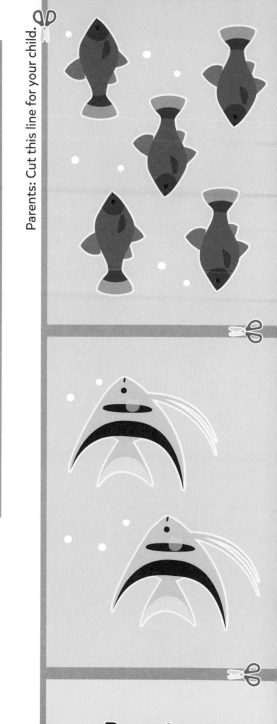

Parents: Cut this line for your child.

Do not use.

THE SPRING

Act in the Play

To Parents: Encourage your child to consider the shapes of the shadows when deciding where each cutout mask belongs. Because shapes may be similar, ask your child which costume has the same color as the mask.

Cut out the masks. Then glue them in place to match each animal costume.

Sticker

Good job!

Glue

Glue

Do not use.

SHOW

PLAY
Friends in the Woods

29

Match the Vehicles

To Parents: This activity is designed to help your child learn how to separate items into groups. Help your child decide which vehicle belongs where by asking, "What is this vehicle called?" or "Does it belong in the sky or in the water?" It is okay if your child places an airplane on the border or in the sea.

Cut out the vehicles. Then glue them in the sky or in the water.

Good job!

Sticker

Parents: Cut these thin lines for your child.

Glue

Glue

Glue

Glue

Glue

Glue

Glue

Glue

Sticker

Good job!

Match the Animals

To Parents: Help your child sort the cutouts into two piles: creatures that belong in the sea and creatures that belong in the sky. Then have your child place the cutouts on the picture before gluing them in place. It is okay if your child places a dolphin on the border or in the sky.

Cut out the animals. Then glue them in the sky or in the water.

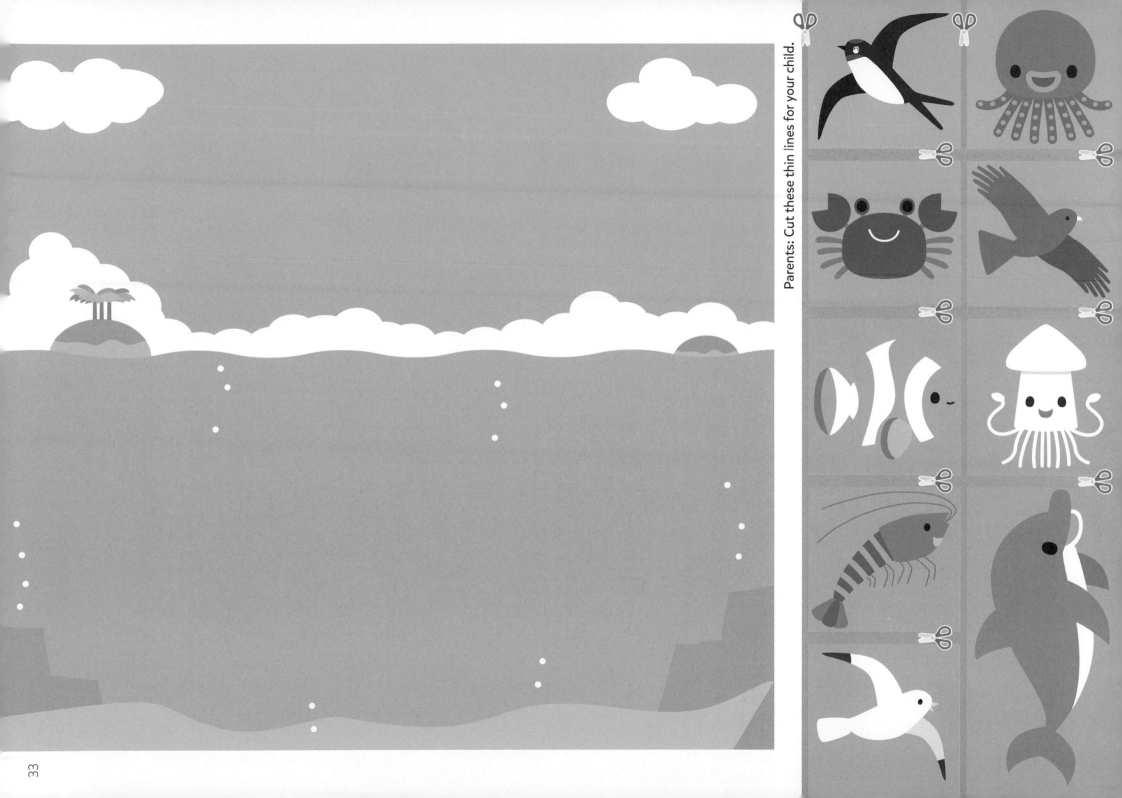

Parents: Cut these thin lines for your child.

Make a Meal

To Parents: Have your child use the food cutouts to make lunch and dinner. Ask, "Which foods would you likely eat for lunch and which would you likely eat for dinner?"

Cut out the foods. Then glue them on the plates to make lunch and dinner.

Glue Glue Glue Glue Glue Glue Glue Glue Glue Glue

Good Job!

Sticker

34

Parents: Cut these thin lines for your child.

Do not use.

Do not use.

Glue	Glue
Glue	Glue
Glue	Glue
Glue	Glue
Do not use.	**Do not use.**

Go to the Haunted House

To Parents: After cutting out the monsters, say their names: vampire, witch, mummy, and skeleton. As they are the same size, your child can glue them in any space. After gluing, ask your child, "Which monster are you the most scared of?"

Sticker

Good job!

Cut out the monsters. Then glue them in the haunted house. Add bat stickers to the spooky sky.

Parents: Cut this line for your child.

Glue

Glue

Glue

Glue

Play Musical Instruments

To Parents: Place the musical instruments on the picture before gluing them in place. Have your child match the pieces by paying attention to the shapes of the instruments and the colors of each child's clothes. If they know some instruments, mimic the sounds as well.

Sticker

Good job!

Cut out the musical instruments. Then glue them on the shadow shapes that match.

MUSIC

CONCERT

Parents: Cut this line for your child.

Put the Cake on the Table

To Parents: In this activity, your child will practice cutting curved lines. Show how to do it, as it may be difficult in the beginning. The secret is cutting while turning the paper, not turning the scissors.

Cut out the plate on page 41 and glue it to the table on this page.
Then cut out the cupcake picture and glue it to the plate.

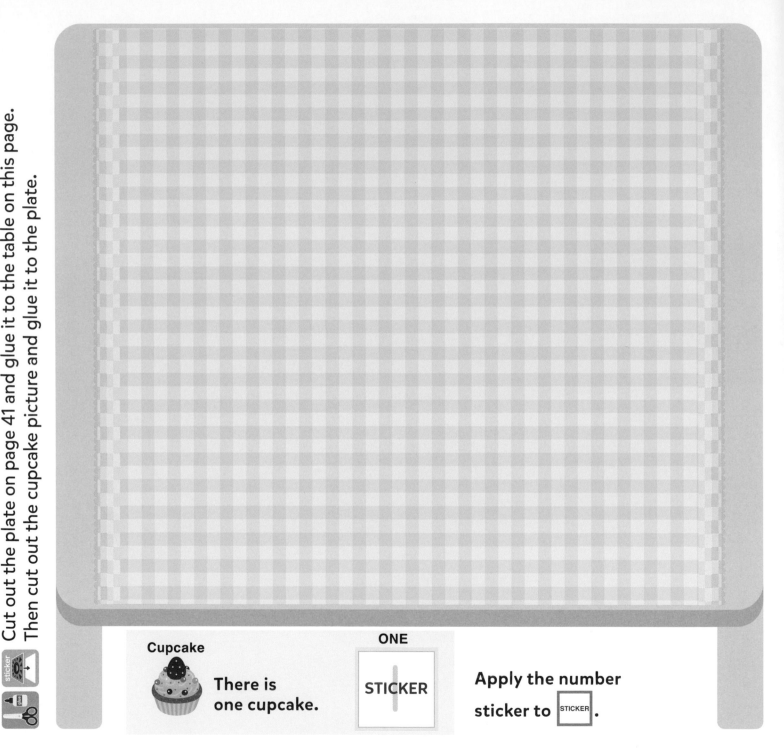

Cupcake

There is one cupcake.

ONE

STICKER

Apply the number sticker to STICKER .

Glue

Glue

Glue

Glue

Glue

Good job!
Sticker

40

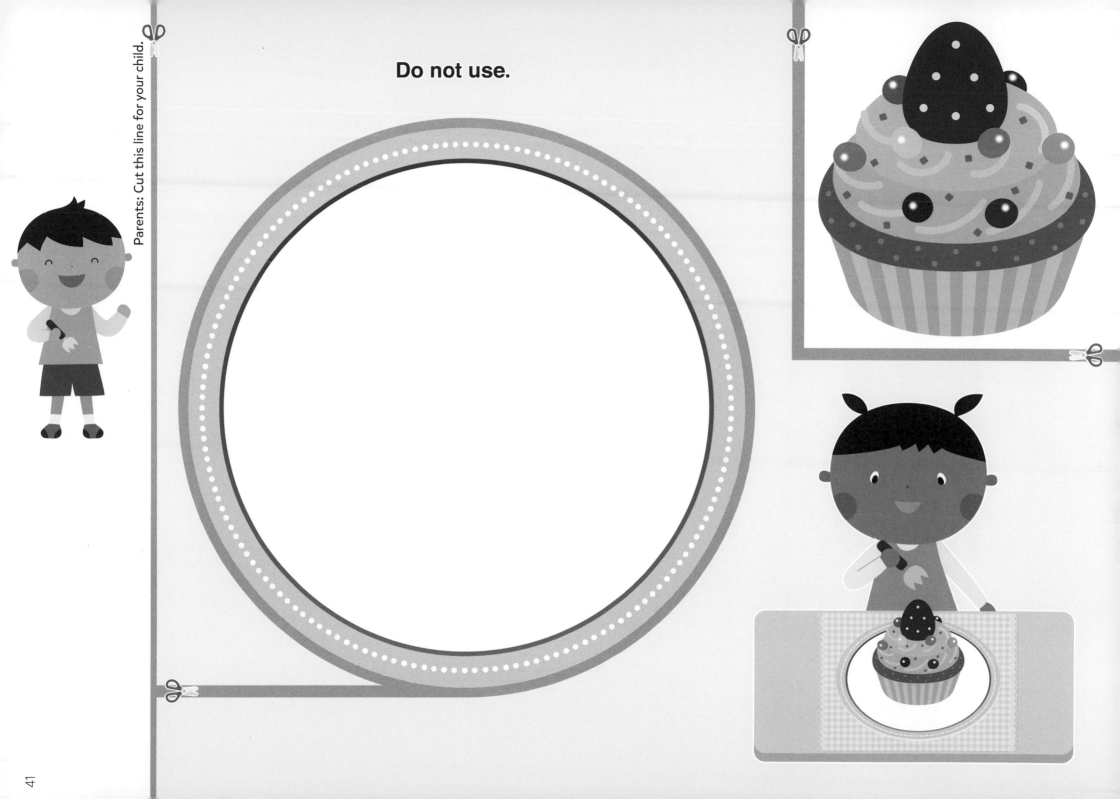

Parents: Cut this line for your child.

Glue

Do not use.

Glue

42

Count the Animals

To Parents: Starting with this activity, your child will practice cutting all lines. After cutting out the animals, count the rabbits and the hamsters. If counting is difficult for your child, help them sort the rabbit and hamster pieces, and glue them to each home.

Cut out the rabbit and hamster pictures. How many rabbits are there? How many hamsters are there? Apply the correct number sticker to each STICKER.

THE RABBITS' HOUSE

There are
two rabbits.

TWO

2

STICKER

There are
three hamsters.

THREE

3

STICKER

THE HAMSTERS' HOUSE

Count the Fruit

To Parents: After cutting out the strawberries and apples, arrange each of them in the basket. Then point to each piece with your fingers, counting as you go.

Cut out the apples and strawberries. Glue them to the basket with the matching fruit. Count each group and apply the correct number sticker to .

There are four apples.

APPLE

FOUR

STICKER

There are five strawberries.

STRAWBERRY

FIVE

5

STICKER

Cut this line first.

Do not use.

Do not use.

Glue

Glue

Glue

Glue

Glue

Glue

Glue

Do not use.

Do not use.

46

Display Toys

To Parents: Have your child glue the toys anywhere on the shelves. Name each toy as they place it. After they're done, praise your child by saying, "You did it by yourself!"

Cut out the toys. Then glue them on the shelves wherever you like.

Do not use.

Do not use.

Glue

Glue

Glue

Glue

Glue

Glue

Do not use.

Do not use.

Who Is Driving?

To Parents: Have your child say the name of the animals and place them wherever they like. After they're done, ask them "What color is the car that the panda is in?"

Good job!

Sticker

The animals are having fun in the cars. Cut out the animals. Then glue them in whichever car you like.

Cut this line first.

Do not use. Do not use.

Glue	Glue
Glue	Glue
Glue	Glue
Glue	Glue
Do not use.	**Do not use.**

Sticker

★ Good job! ★

Let's Celebrate

To Parents: This activity teaches one-to-one correspondence. Have your child place the balloon pieces on the paper. Then say, "Let's give a balloon to each boy and girl." Make sure your child doesn't place the pieces in the wrong direction.

Cut out the balloons. Then glue them wherever you like.

Cut this line first.

51

Glue

Glue

Glue

Glue

Glue

Sticker

★ Good Job! ★

Put Things Away

To Parents: Explain that each item belongs with others of its kind. Have your child use this information to decide where each item should be placed and glued. Talk about how important it is to put things away after you are done using them.

Let's put the things back where they belong.
Cut out each item and glue it on the picture where you think it should be.

Cut this line first.

Put the Backpacks Away

To Parents: Pay attention to the animal on each backpack. Then have your child use this information to decide where each backpack belongs. Talk about how children often get their own cubbyhole in school where they can keep their personal belongings.

Sticker

Good job!

54

Let's help clean the classroom. Cut out the backpacks. Then glue each into the matching cubbyhole.

Cut this line first.

Glue

Glue

Glue

Glue

Glue

Sticker

★ Good job! ★

Finish the Puzzle

To Parents: In this activity, your child will practice cutting longer lines. Your child should keep the scissors open and close them only slightly to make short cuts at the base of the scissors, without closing the scissors all the way. Show them how to move the scissors by cutting only at the base.

Cut out the puzzle pieces on the page 57.
Then glue them in place to match the rabbit picture on this page.

Cut this line first.

Do not use.

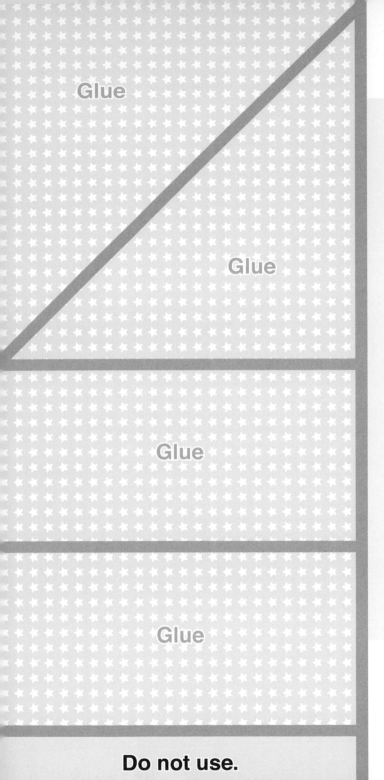

Glue

Glue

Glue

Glue

Do not use.

Wash Our Hands

To Parents: In this activity, your child will practice putting glue on only part of the paper. Make sure that your child puts the glue on the blue star box, not the cutout. Use this activity to teach children handwashing!

Sticker

Good job!

Cut out the towel and faucet pictures. Then glue them on the correct blue star box.

Wash hands.

Glue

Hang the towel up.

Glue

Dry hands.

Cut this line first.

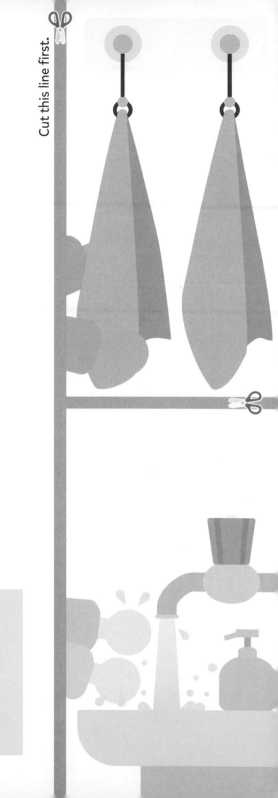

Make the Animals Dance

To Parents: In this activity, your child will practice cutting just partway through the paper. To be able to stop cutting at the right place, your child should practice making short cuts only at the base of the scissors until they reach the end of the line.

Good job!

Sticker

Cut along the gray lines to make legs. Then glue the red legs to the octopus and the yellow legs to the squid. Move their legs and make them dance.

Glue

Glue

How to Play

After gluing on the legs, curl them.

Hold the paper and shake it to see the octopus dance.

Repeat the process with the squid.

Cut this line first.

Make the Animals Laugh

To Parents: In this activity, your child will practice cutting curved lines. As shown on page 40, practice cutting while moving the paper. To make it more challenging, fold each shape in half and cut. Cutting two layers of paper is also good practice

Cut along the gray lines and glue the shapes to the matching animal. Apply the eye stickers. Open and close Hippo's and Frog's mouths to make them laugh.

Good job!

Sticker

Apply

Apply

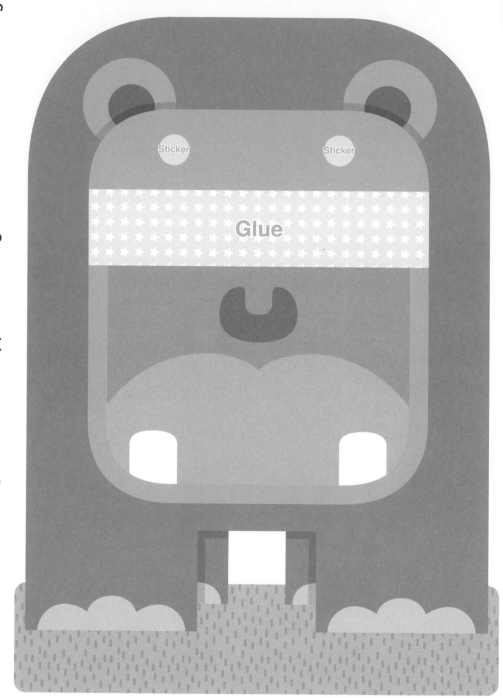

Sticker   Sticker

Glue

Sticker

Sticker

Glue

Cut this line first.

Do not use.

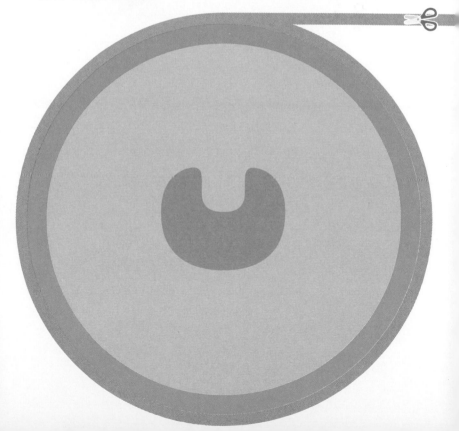

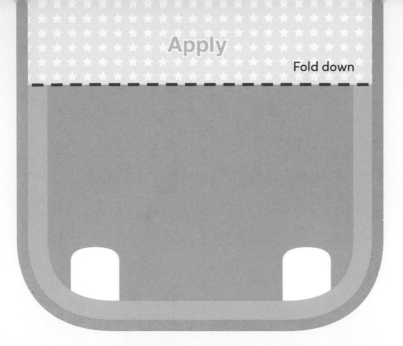

Apply

Fold down

Do not use.

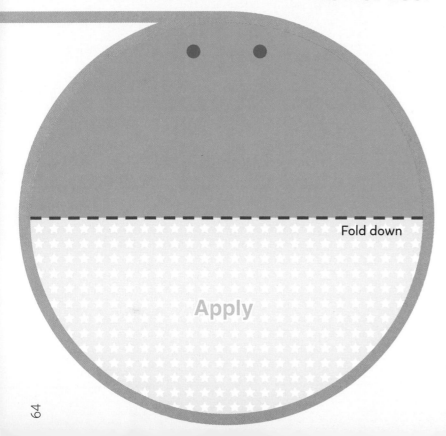

Fold down

Apply

How to Play

Hippo

1. Cut out the piece, then fold down along ■■■■ to make it flat.

2. Glue onto the orange star area.

3. Apply eye stickers to Sticker.

4. Open and close Hippo's mouth to make him laugh.

Frog

1. Cut out the piece, then fold down along ■■■■ to make it flat.

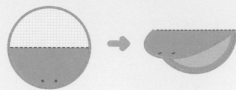

2. Glue onto the orange star area.

3. Apply eye stickers to Sticker.

4. Open and close Frog's mouth to make her laugh.